plantfirmations

plantfirmations

Isaac Fanjiang Carrillo

Sofia Carrillo

Porcelain Books

plantfirmations

"You, yourself, as much as anybody in the entire universe, deserve your love and affection."

— Buddha

plantfirmations

plantfirmations

I am Safe and Secure

When we go through life we often feel unstable. Its important to remember that it's only temporary. You will find peace.

I have faith in my inner guidance...
I am
Not Afraid to
Follow it

When we feel lost we must remember to trust in ourselves. You will find a way.

I know that I am headed in the
Right
Direction

Some times we are unsure of our own trajectory. It can be scary. Just remember, you are headed to the right place.

New Environments

I am not afraid to put myself into

New places can be scary. Leaving your comfort zone takes courage.

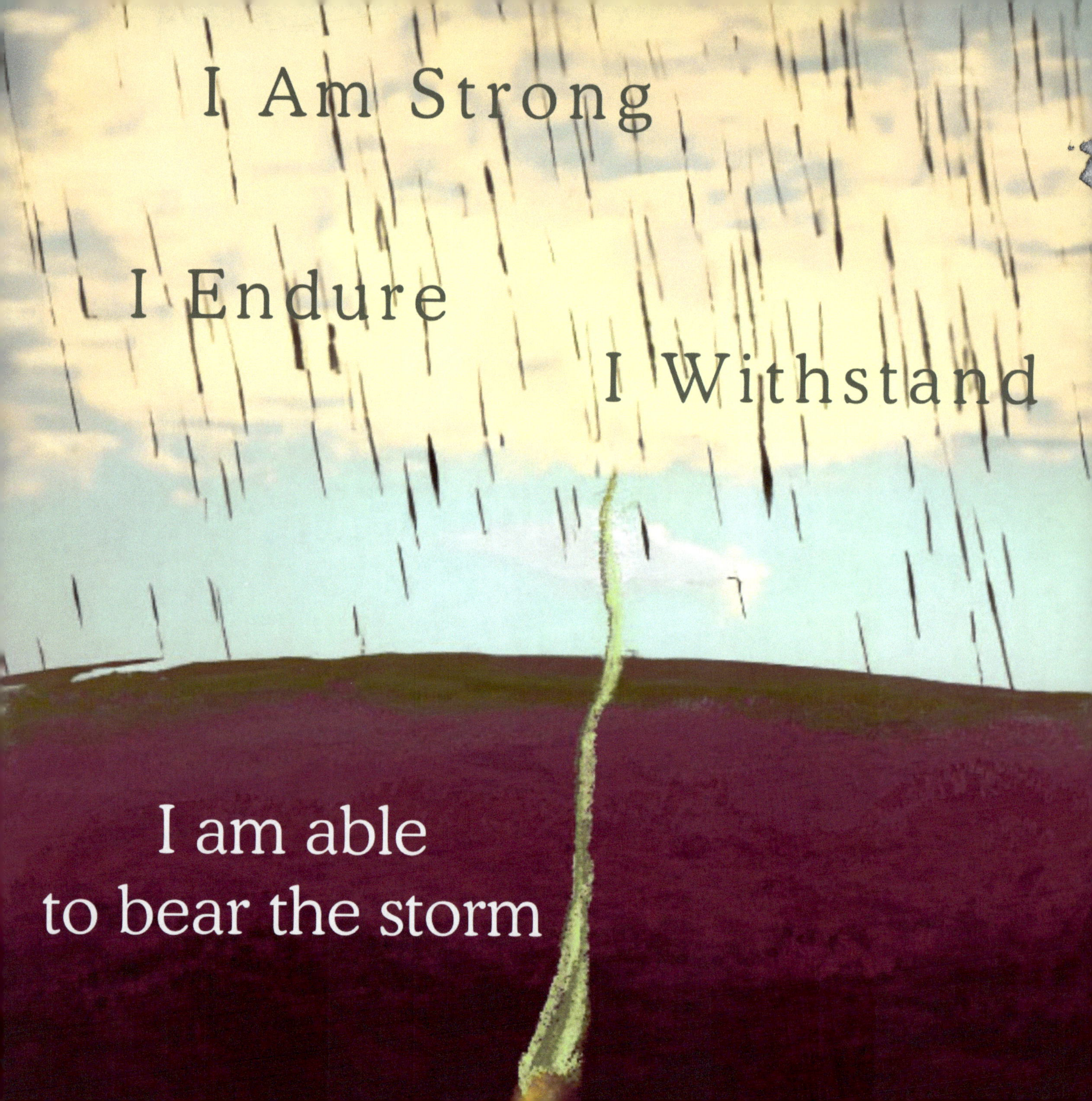
I Am Strong
I Endure
I Withstand
I am able
to bear the storm

There will always be some rainy days. But the clouds make us appreciate the sun.

I am always
Growing
I am always
Improving

Sometimes you can be unhappy with your situation or even with yourself. But we are all on a path of growth.

I am
Seen

Sometimes we feel invisible.
But you are being seen for who you are.

You are being recognized

I am Beautiful

We are each beautiful in our own ways. We don't have to strive to be anything other than ourselves. You are beautiful.

I am capable of
existing with
others

It can feel easier on your own.
It can feel like you can't interact
with other people.
But the presence of others doesn't
drag you down.
It lifts you up.

I am
Me

"Promise me you'll always remember: You're braver than you believe, and stronger than you seem, and smarter than you think."
(Christopher Robin from Winnie the Pooh)

- A.A. Milne

About the author

Isaac Fanjiang Carrillo

Isaac Carrillo is a high schooler attending Horace Greeley High school. A sophmore in 10th grade, Isaac is passionate about mental health and psychology.

"While experiencing some of the most stressful years of our lives, we realized that others probably feel the same. We created this book as an aide for anybody who feels stressed in any situation."
- Isaac Carrillo

plantfirmations